From the
PUDDLE
to the
POND

A Collection of Short Poems/Stories

From the PUDDLE to the POND

BERTRAM SMITH

Reflections of My Life's Journey
in the Bahamas and America

ISBN: 978-1-950685-39-4

Contents

Dedication

This book is dedicated to all those strong women and men in my life—too many to mention, but I would be remiss if I did not mention a few. This is for my late mother, Ruth Smith, my four sisters, Lucy Taylor, Jane Johnson, Edith Evans-Seymour, and Ruthnell Bull, and all of my aunts, Auntie Manda, Auntie Lillis, Auntie Lue, Auntie Macy, and Auntie Gwennie. These are women who raised me, molded me, nurtured me, and even disciplined me. I have so many stories—fond memories of all of them—the telling of these stories could go on for days. I have to admit, my aunt Gwendolyn Forbes, "Auntie Grenny," as we called her, could bake the best "light-bread" on South Andros, part of the reason we loved stopping at her house after school to pay a visit and show our respects.

I also dedicate this book to my Father, Byron "Beerun" Smith, who indeed taught me all that he knew and could. I dedicate it also to my brother, William Smith, "Rasta Willie," who raised me as a son during my rough teenage years, and who also taught me many life lessons.

I dedicate this book, also, to my two daughters, Falashade and Jamani—two of the most beautiful young people I know. They help to keep me 'straight' and grounded. Finally, I dedicate this book to my beautiful, darling of a wife, Leslie. She is the love of my life and forever will be one of my greatest inspirations.

Foreword

"From the Puddle to the Pond" is a journey through enlightenment. This book contains an eclectic collection of poems spanning two diverse countries.

There's something heartwarming, inspirational, and thought-provoking for everyone. Above all, the contents of this book addresses all facets of humanity—God, family, love, humor, and important life lessons.

As you read this poetic rendition, you will experience the eventful educational, spiritual, and personal development of its highly respected and acclaimed author.

Immerse yourself in the insightful nature of the author's words, and you will expand and brighten your horizons.

Ruthnell Bull
Retired Public School Administrator
Principal of New Direction Christian Academy
Statesboro, Georgia

Introduction

I never thought I would be writing a book. Growing up in the Bahamas and, on the island of Andros, perhaps the least developed island in our archipelago, a young man simply did not have such lofty aspirations.

I have always loved the written word, however. Introduced to books at a very early age, as I shared in one of my pieces, I believe, books—the written word--actually saved my life. I first became aware of my knack for writing around about the fifth or sixth grade. In sixth grade, one of my teachers, Alphonso Adderley, presented an essay that I had written in Religious Studies to our head teacher of the all age school at Kemp's Bay as validation that I, along with another student, were ready to sit for the all-important Bahamas Junior Certificate (BJC) exams.

Of course there were other promptings--encouragement, I call them--along the way. None convincing enough, I hasten to add, to make me go: "Umm, maybe I should become a writer."

In 1976, I was accepted into the College of the Bahamas (now the University of the Bahamas). I, along with several dozen other students from the "Out Islands"—less developed outer islands in the Bahamas—were let in as a kind of experiment, to see if we could survive academically alongside other students from New Providence, many of whom had attended the much more prestigious schools—schools such as Government High, St. Augustine, St. Johns, Aquinas, and Queens College.

I have to admit it was a boost to my ego to see that, not only could I survive, but that I could also hold my own and even thrive in such a rigorous and challenging academic environment. This was a very impressionable time of my life and development, yet nothing was leading me to think that I would become an author. Yet, there were signs. On more than one occasion, lecturers at the college would select my writings--mainly composition and essays at the time—to share with the class.

I could never forget such professors like Mr. George Wilson and Dr. Melvin Rahming who praised my work and encouraged me to continue down the path of learning, growing, and expanding my horizons.

Dr. Rahming, in particular, encouraged me to go beyond the Bahamas, and immerse myself, he would say, in the larger currents of life and learning.

In 1980, I was blessed with the opportunity to further my education in the United States, where I experienced my first real taste of success with writing.

In my first class at the University of South Florida--a Narration and Description class--the professor scribbled three topics on the board, asked us to respond to one of them, then promptly left the room. I remember writing a short piece about a woman who lived in the suburbs--a soap opera addict--who was so obsessed with an episode of her daily "drug" that she was undisturbed by all the commotion that was taking place in her neighborhood one fateful day. She was so fixated, obsessed with her program, that she missed the fire that swept through her neighborhood, all the wailing sirens of police and fire engines, even the scorching of her own house.

A couple of days later, the professor returned our corrected and graded work—all, except mine and another student's.

He called us up to the front at the end of the class after all the other students had filed out, praised the other student, and dismissed her.

Then, he turned to me and said,

"Hey, Bertram, tell me something: Where are you from?"

"I'm from the Caribbean," I said, thinking perhaps that's all he knew.

"Yeah, yeah," he responded, "I kind of figured that, but--where from in the Caribbean?"

"The Bahamas," I said, sheepishly.

Then he said something that changed my life forever! He said: "Hey, Bertram, let me tell you something! You know, Bertram, you are smarter, much smarter, than all of these American kids."

Professor Ginzberg's words changed my life, not because I believed him, or thought he was being one hundred percent honest and sincere with me. Those words changed my life because, for the first time, I could see a glimmer of my place in the world. For the first time ever, I thought, this little black boy, who was from Smith's Hill, South Andros, in the Bahamas...

Those words... They made me feel, for the first time, like I belonged.

I am from…

I am from the island of Andros
Andros is home to me
Swimming in the blue hole
Running
Playing
Frolicking with my friends along white sandy beaches
The ever-present sounds of seagulls
Hovering
Barking hysterically
As the local fishermen tend their catch
I am from Andros
Short walk to the ocean
The cool crisp breeze
Swimming in the crystal clear blue waters
Playing stick-ball with old stuffed socks in the crossroad
I am from Andros,
Splashing through shallow waters
Skipping
Yelling
Running
Pointing
Jabbing my finger with excitement
At the dark 'cloud'
Stealthily gliding through the crystal-clear blue waters

Yes
I am from the island of Andros
A flurry of people
Mostly women and children
Running down the beach
The quick unfurling of the nets
A small quiet frenzy of excitement in the shimmering heat
Wading through the waters
Shielding their eyes to see the advancing shadow
Serious-looking
All business
Bobbing up and down in the water
Encircling
Children
Bobbing in the water as they run
Laughing
Gamboling
Splashing water to drive the shadow into the nets
I am from Andros
Slowly encircling them
They have them cornered
Furiously
The children
Mature for their ages
Splash water
Slapping
To drive them deeper into the net
Focused

Dead serious
Calculating
Closing off all escape
The women
Experts at their craft
Close off all escape
Briefly
For just one flashing moment
If you blink you will miss it
Cracking that trade mark Bahamian-woman smile
Mission accomplished
Dragging the strained and bulging net to shore
I am from Andros
Silvery fish
Thousands
Spill out onto the white sand
Littering the ground
Flapping
Kicking up sand
Gasping their final breaths
Tubs
They filled them to the brim with fluttering fish and seawater
When it's all said and done
Everyone gets a share
I am from Andros
Going fishing with daddy and 'Lisha
On cool quiet peaceful Saturday mornings
The waves lapping at the shore

Quick glimpses of the colorful fish as they dart to and fro
Brushing against the just as colorful coral fans and quickly
gliding out of view
I am from Andros,
Shooting marbles in the street
A grown-up yelling
You children, what's the matter with you'll
Are you'll out of you'll's minds or just trying to get killed
I am from Andros
In church, three times on Sunday
And almost every night of the week
Walking a straight line
Since everybody knows we're the pastor's children and need to
set an example
I am from Andros
Where they stumble out into the street at night
In the summer time
Still tired from the night before
To catch crabs
Roast corns
And tell Ole Bro' Bookie and Bro' Rabbie stories
It is true
I am from that place
Growing up and running bare-foot over sharp limestone rocks,
The few tourists who come say
How do you do it
Those rocks they don't hurt your feet
No sir we say
This is where we from
Andros is my home

Scaling the fence to raid somebody's fruit trees
Mango, dilly, sugar apples, plums, sour sops, and guineps
To us
They are all fair game
My father says
Boys
Stay out of them people's yard
Don't you'll have you'll own yard to play up in
But that's no fun
I am from Andros
Sitting beneath the old tamarind tree
Dogs barking
Men smoking pipes and slamming dominoes
While the women are left to do the back-breaking work
Girls walking down the street
Looking prim and proper
Laughing
Their mouths cupped behind their hands
I am from that place called Andros
Dogs always barking
The ever smell of outdoor cooking corns roasting smoke fire
burning
Children playing in the street
Yes
I am from the island of Andros
Andros is home to me
Andros
That sun-drenched land
Where it rains sometimes in the summer time
And the coconut trees sway gently in the sweet cool breeze

The Islands of the Bahamas

Captivating
Intriguing
They too are home to me
Radiating calm
Peace
Serenity
joy
Millions of people come
They brag about the islands' breath-taking beauty
Their charm
They are paradise they say
What amazes me though
Is how a million people can look at something
And miss the most important thing
Its most outstanding feature
The real beauty
The essence of the thing
The beauty of this place
As far as I am concerned
Is not the sand
Sea
Or sky

The beauty of this place
To me
Is locked up in a smile
That is the real charm
It's not the beaches
The water
It is that smile
Natural and pure
Hides all the pain
It outshines the sun
More beautiful than the crystal clear blue waters
Yet
Like the sun on cloudy days
It doesn't come out often
But when it does
Oh man when it does
The true beauty of the islands of the Bahamas
To me
Is that smile
Natural and pure
Hides all the pain
Outshines the Bahamian sun
More beautiful and alluring and captivating than sun sky or
waters
Yet
Like the sun
It is not flighty or fake
It doesn't come out often

But when it does
Oh Man when it does
The true beauty of the Islands of the Bahamas
Its real charm
Its magic
Is the beauty of a Bahamian woman's smile

Desire

Her Grammy
Since that is what she called her
Said no black man
Was good enough for her Grand-daughter
She was from one of those islands
Where her family still clung to some long held traditions
She used to own and run a liquor store
Somewhere Over the Hill
She would say
Son who your people
Where you from
Which island
Back there
In our small world
Those were loaded questions
Telling
Meant to be revealing
And to reveal
Then I would say
Ma'am I am from Andros
From Andros she would go
Andros
Lord have mercy
What's in Andros except a whole bunch of snakes and crabs

Her Grand-daughter was light
Could pass for white
We were both young
In search of something we both hope we would eventually find
We were always together
She said I was different
Not like the boys her family approved
And approved of
She said she just wanted to be free
Someday leave this puddle
Said she was sick and tired of living her life in a bubble
They tried
But no matter how hard they tried
They could not pry her away from me

Through the Streets of Nassau

Through the streets of Nassau
We would go
Me and my baby just going for a ride
Always in a hurry
With no need to worry
Enjoying the ride
Sharing a world
Made
It seemed
Just for the two of us

Out through the wide gates of The College
And onto the Boulevard
Free of books
Finally
Up Wulff Road
Past the theater
Where we would sometimes retreat to escape the summer heat
Past the bad boys sitting idly on the blocks
Then quickly onto Mackey
Sometimes down Poincietta
Always ending up on Bay

Me and my baby just going for a ride
Always in a hurry
With no need to worry
Enjoying the ride
Sharing a world
Made
It seemed
Just for the two of us

A quick turn on Shirley
and into traffic
Horns honking
Sometimes blaring
reckless motor bikes dangerously weaving
Motorist yelling
Sometimes
An insignificant voice would yell out my name
And she would say who's that
Nobody I would say
Finally we get back to Bay
All roads
It seems
lead that way
This time we are heading out East to Potter's Cay
A little windy
The cool crisp air
Flirting with her hair
And the zesty smell of the sea-fish-and-conch

Mingled with an array of other loud scents
Enough to take your breath away
Some talking
Laughing
Others looking sad
The voices sometimes muffled
As we speed on by
Me and my baby just going for a ride
Always In a hurry
With no need to worry
Enjoying the ride
Sharing a world
Made
It seemed
Just for the two of us

Under the bridge
She says slow down plenty of pot-holes out here
And could we get some fruits
An endless array of fruits and vegetables stalls
Too many to choose from
Women sitting
Some standing
Counting money
Making change
Laughing
Talking
Telling jokes

Fruits and vegetables

Of every description

Fresh in from the neighboring islands

Colorful bright and sweet-looking

Mangoes

Bananas

Guineps

Hog Plums

Scarlet plums

Sugar apples

Sour-sop

Tamarind

Jelly Coconuts

Dried ones too

Oranges

Sour oranges

Limes

Melons

Pa paw

Yams

Cassava

Sweet potatoes

Pigeon peas

Beans

All neatly arranged

Crabs crawling out of and all over baskets

Crabs in wire mesh jostling wrestling and clawing each other

Black crabs

White crabs
Today she says she feels like mangoes and guineps
Can I try one she asks the lady and are they real sweet
They real sweet the lady says judge for yourself
They both laughed
Then as if it was contagious
A ripple of laughter rang out from behind all the other stalls
under the bridge
Easing into traffic
We speed up again
Only to slow down where the mail-boats come in
We stop to watch the melee
Mail boats getting larger as they come closer
People and cargo
Dangling dangerously from all sides
Men scurrying along the dock
Lunging for ropes as they are flung
Squawking at each other
Finally
Ropes fastened
Weary passengers disembarking
After a while
The noise dies down
I want to stay and watch a little while longer
But she says let's go
And since she too is sweet-looking
I say okay let's go
We leave the seagulls still squawking and yelling

Back in the direction of Bay
Through the streets of Nassau
Me and my baby just going for a ride
Always in a hurry
With no need to worry
Enjoying the ride
Sharing a world
Made
it seemed
Just for the two of us

Back on Bay
And back into traffic
Congestion everywhere
Some in a hurry
Shoppers strolling leisurely in and out of stores
Tourists
Lawyers
Bankers
Women
Young and old they work in the banks
Students
Decked out smartly in their school uniforms
And everywhere tourists
Some looking lost
Some bemused and slightly bewildered
A policeman on his box
Majestic looking

In his crisp policeman suit
Directing
Or attempting to direct the unresponsive traffic
A young police woman
Beautiful
Yet no time to smile
Crosses the street
Only she could stop the traffic
Finally we hit the bend to go out West
We speed up again
Windows down
Again the cool breeze flirting with her hair
Past the Drum Beat
The pier
The cruise ships nestled in the harbor
We stop at Arawak Cay
Just for a moment
Long enough to munch on Crack-conch and share a Goombay
She laughs and says
You forgot to get the straw
Back on the road
Headed out West
Honking cars
Busses and Jitneys clogging the street
Irate drivers yelling
Their hands a flurry of motions
Sometimes we would come too close
Have to swerve

Excuse me I would shout into the air
And she would laugh and say
Are we going for a swim today
Through the streets of Nassau
Me and my baby just going for a ride
Always in a hurry
With no need to worry
Enjoying the ride
Sharing a world
Made
it seemed
Just for the two of us
Through the streets of Nassau
Young wild and free

Moon Over Nassau Harbor

There was a time
Long gone now
When you could go with the one you love
To the secluded spots around Nassau Harbor
You could sit
Someplace like out on Arawak Cay
Watch the lights
All different colors
Reflecting off the water
Watch the ships off in the distance
Lit up
All impressive and majestic
This was a time
Seems long ago now
When you could sit quietly on Saunders Beach
Or Goodman's Bay
Down by Compass Point
Or even Delaporte
Those were the days
A time when one Chicken-in-the-Bag was good enough
for two
Wash them down with a couple of Goombay

I always like mine better without the straw
I still like to go
Travel back there
At least I can still conjure it up
Try to preserve what has been lost
I think I'll go back there just one more time…
Ah, there was a time
Long gone now
When you could go with the one you love
To the secluded spots around Nassau Harbor
And you could sit
Someplace like out on Arawak Cay
Watch the lights
All different colors
Reflecting off the water
Watch the ships off in the distance
Lit up
All impressive
And majestic

A Summer Romance

She came from like out of nowhere
One day
That summer
She just showed up
She and her Jehovah's Witness family
At 16 my first thought
My only thought was
Did she like boys
The island had never seen the likes of her
American girl
Hot pants and tee-shirt
Curvaceous
Vivacious
Enough to drive my mom insane
As far as my mom was concerned
They all spelled trouble
Were too fresh and too forward
None good enough for her baby boy
Cindy
that was her name
Cindy
The girl from Michigan
She brought a whole new dimension to my mom's paranoia
So when my mom heard that we were somewhere

Talking in the dark
She just flipped a switch
Told me to get home to an empty house
There was no one home and the house was unguarded
Cindy innocently said let me go with you
Now why would she want to go say a thing like that
She just didn't understand
My mom turned to molten ash
Cindy did not understand
She didn't understand Island life
And she certainly didn't understand out-island mothers
She had even given me Sudafed when I had told her my mom
was sick
She had tried to talk to her
But girls were where my mom drew the line
They were just a non-negotiable
In her eyes
They all spelled trouble
Were too fresh and too forward
None good enough for her baby boy
One thing on their minds she said
And she didn't care whether they were black or white
Local
Or came from afar

Sunset In the Back of Aunt Peetrul's Yard

Aunt Peetrul's yard
Sat up on top of the hill
In Smith's Hill
The perfect place to sit and watch the sun go down
The perfect quiet spot to think
Dream
Let your mind just wander freely
Aunt Peetrul was my daddy's sister
The only one I really knew
The islands of the Bahamas could not contain her
She was just too beautiful
Aunt Peetrul left
Wanted to experience life across the ocean
Life she said in the Bahamas
Was too much like swimming in the shallows
Now the weeds and shrubs and prickly grass grew freely
The chinnie-briers
That if you are not careful
Would reach out and grab you and wouldn't let go
They all had sprung up and almost taken over the yard
Jumbay
Bajerina

Soracee,
All good for healing
Grew wild and for the most part undisturbed
Off in the distance grew the kamalame and lignum whitey
Strong tall and sturdy
Snake-like vines and moss now covered them
As the sun went down they could play tricks with your eyes
Make you believe you were seeing giant dark-green ghosts
A few stray dogs and cats still stroll
Still called the place home
They were content
Or so it seemed
To share this half-wild and secluded spot with me
Here
I would sit and watch the sun go down
Listen to and relish the quiet
Bask and bathe in the view
The silver sunlight streaming
Through the leaves and the branches of the dilly trees
Off in the distance
Faint
Dogs barking
Children playing
Cousin Susan
Calling for Reggie and David to come home
Once in a while a weary rooster sounded
All else is quiet
Here in my own tropical wilderness of a garden

It seemed like the world was at perfect peace
This is where I first learned respect and reverence for God
Sometimes
As the sun slowly crept out of view
I would whisper…
Thank you God
For giving me this place
To sit and contemplate
The wonders of you and your glorious works
To see
In the sunset
That blaze of radiant hues
A fleeting moment
Red
Yellow
Purple and blue
Orange too
All Screaming
Yet another proclamation of you

What Daddy Taught Us

Daddy taught us everything he knew and could
Didn't have much of a formal education
Sent to work harvesting sponges
He was needed to help with feeding the family
But I will never forget my dad
For all that he taught us
What Daddy taught us
Daddy taught us everything he knew and could

Cool quiet lazy Saturday mornings
Daddy would say
Boys we going fishing
Hard work
Daddy would say
If a man doesn't want to work he shouldn't eat
And his voice would carry
Echo in the calm still morning
As we gently shoved the little dinghy into the yet undisturbed
waters
The only sounds
Other than my daddy's voice
Directing
Teaching us
Would be the waves

Gently lapping at the shore
A few crabs for bait
The wooden looking glass to see the conchs
Nestled in their beds below on the dark-green carpeted floor
Be careful
Look out now Daddy would say
You want to keep the head pointed into the waves
Ease into the boat
Sit toward the middle
Always stay seated when you in a boat
As we glide further into the deep
The boat rocking
Gliding
Gently side to side
From the motion of my daddy sculling
He would say
Don't put your hands in that water
The water that looks tempting and ever so inviting
So clear
You could mistake it for glass
And you can see all the way through
What Daddy taught us
Daddy taught us everything he knew and could

Born out of wedlock
Stained and shunned because he was the family's shame
The shoal
That big dark shadow in the water

Fast approaching

Smash just one fin at a time Daddy would say

You don't need to use the whole thing

The fish just need a taste

Check your line

Make sure you have the right size hook and sinker

We drop anchor

My daddy always the teacher

Would say

When you throw

You throw it so

Watch your brother's head

No

You can't throw it on the shoal

Throw it off to the side

Like so

What Daddy taught us

Daddy taught us everything he knew and could

Never learned to read or write

Yet he could read the Bible from cover to cover

Both my dad and my mom were business people

Daddy caught the mail-boat

Went to Nassau every month

To hawk his wares

Coconuts

Fruits

And "medicine"

That is how he supported the family
Check to make sure the anchor took he would say
Make sure it fastened real-good
As the boat's head bobbed gently up and down in the water
When no fish biting in one spot
You just want to go to the next
If you feeling sick drink a little sea-water
Wait for the tug
Now strike
Don't pull too fast
But keep the slack out of the line
If it's a grouper
He aint going to fight you
Mutton fish is more feisty
Bonefish they will run all day
What Daddy taught us
Daddy taught us everything he knew and could

Man of staunch faith
And doting husband
That was just the kind of man my daddy was
Take the staff in your right hand
Take the glass in your left
Now make sure you hook 'em good
Once the giant conch's in the boat Daddy would say
Grab the hammer
you going to give it just a few small taps
The shell soft right there

So you don't have to hit hard
Now shove with the back of the hammer
Take your hand and pull
Twist it and it will slide right out
What Daddy taught us
Daddy taught us everything he knew and could

Daddy could scull boat like no other
Making it jerk and lurch through the sometimes choppy seas
Strong
Big hands good for gripping the oar
Sometimes he would use the staff
The one for hooking the conchs
He would slide the limber staff
Pressing it along the side of the boat
Causing the boat to move forward in long smooth strides
And the coconut and the grape trees would walk backwards
As we glide and rode the waves all the way home
One day Daddy just said
come
Today you are going to learn to scull
Keep the oars in the hole
Use your wrist
You don't have to fight it
Just get your timing down
There you go
What Daddy taught us
Daddy taught us everything he knew and could

Pastor of the local Church of God
Daddy was always there
Most of the time alone
Kneeling at the altar
Loved God and his Family
And
A little bit of American jazz on quiet Sunday afternoons
Daddy would say
Okay now let the boat come to a complete stop
Never jump in the water without looking
A stingray could be buried right there in the sand
Always keep the boat straight
Never take your eyes off the waves
Then Daddy would look at his two young pupils
Flushed and brimming with pride
Well look at that
You boys done real good for yourselves today
And my brother
Who was only three years older
I was ten
would look back up at the teacher
He too would be flushed and beaming with pride
And he would go
Look Daddy
We caught a little bit of everything
Grouper
Yeller tail
Snapper

Mutton fish

Hamlet

Terbit

Red snapper

Angel fish

Hog fish

Rock Fish

Even a barracuda

What Daddy taught us

Like I said

Daddy taught us everything he knew and could .

"Hellcat"

There was this boy

Growing up

He lived in Kemp's Bay

We never knew his name

We just called him Hellcat

Hellcat never went to school

No one knew what he did

Or where he went during the daytime

But every day

Just like clockwork

When we would be coming home from school

Hellcat would meet us

And if we didn't have something he could take

He and his couple of friends

Just as menacing

Just as tough

Would pault* us with rock

Every day was the same old story

They would emerge like Robin Hood

And his band of merry men

Only in reverse

Demand ransom

And if we had none to pay

They would melt away through the trees and into the bushes

Then would come the hail of rocks
One day Hellcat came to the settlement where we lived
He had made friends with my older brother
It was strange to see him with the scowl gone from his face
Laughing playing splashing through the water
They fried the fish they had caught
Lounged beneath the old tamarind tree
Blades of prickly grass dangling from their mouths
The next day
When we had to walk the gauntlet again
Same as before
Hellcat and his gang
Like clockwork
Emerged
Stood before us
Blocking our path
But this time he held up his right arm
Snapped his fingers
Motioned to the small scowling gang around him
The scowls melted from their faces
They seemed disappointed
Leave them alone he said
This here is Willie's brother
He was good to me
Later we learned that Hellcat was adopted
Came from Nassau
Lilly and the Valley Corner
Didn't know his parents

Had never been to school
Spent all day walking splashing in the shallow waters
Didn't really speak to the elderly couple with whom he lived
They just let him be
Hellcat had to find something to do
Something to kill the time I guess
So he chose terrorizing little kids

What She Said

I saw her many years later
We talked
Reminisced
Asked her if she remembered the time
When we were traveling on the mail-boat
From South Andros to Nassau
Two young teenagers
Experimenting with "devilish" thoughts
With a hint of a smile and a twinkle in her eyes
Said she did and what about it

I said
how come you wouldn't kiss me
Even after I begged and pleaded for what seemed like an eternity
Above the din of the engines
As the boat pitched and slammed
Through the rough seas
Smiling
She said she had to go
But before she left
She cast one last glance back at me
Still with that hint of a smile and the twinkle in her eyes
She said
You should've just shut up and kissed me that's all

One of the First Lessons
I Learned in America

One of the first lessons I learned in America
A white woman can be trouble
Especially down south
She saw me first
Said I reminded her of Sidney Poitier
And didn't he come from the same place
We were both working in the restaurant
She was a cashier
It was my job to clean the floors
Take out the trash
I was a poor struggling student at the time
I would see her looking at me
Through the corner of my eye
Even as she counted the money real slow
One night we were alone
Just playing around
It was late
She came to me
She pushed me
Playfully
I was not raised to see skin color
I shoved her back

I thought it was just two people playing around
She said mind you I call the cops
I said do it then
Just like that
The next thing I knew she had called the cops
Luckily for me the cops called my boss
My boss
A quiet decent white man
Loved me like a son
Said he had never met a young man
With such manners and strong work ethic
My boss told the cops that that was a lie
A made-up story
Something about attempted rape
My boss told the cops
If anyone's doing the raping
It would be that hussy
The cops didn't come to arrest me
The cops said that's what they figured
The next day she showed up
Wearing a smile
Told me to hop in
But my boss had already told me
Be careful with these white women
Especially down south

Another Lesson I Learned Shortly Thereafter

In America
As a black man
You will get labeled a lot
People telling you what you can and cannot do
Always trying to set the bar
You get sick of it
Especially if all your life you have never known limitations
Never been taught it
Or not having experienced it
I remember one time I went to work
In a restaurant
Another restaurant
They made me the back-a-the-house manager
Because I could run circles around everyone else working there
But there came a time when I wanted to move up
Be promoted
I had seen the other managers up front
Dressed up
Interacting with the customers
I wanted to have an experience like that
So I sat down with my boss
Told him of my plans

The man had the nerve to ask me what more did I want
And didn't I know
I was already the highest paid back-a-the-house manager in
the country
I could see he missed my point
His perception of me was obviously skewed
Soon afterwards I gave my two weeks' notice
If there is one thing in life you have to learn
It's that when others say you can't
You have to dig in
Let dogged determination show them you can

The Girl from Argentina

She was in my English class at the university
I was now an instructor
She was one of my students
She spoke very little English
She was vivacious
Full of passion
Full of life
She wanted to know if I was going to the party
She said I should go out with her sometime
That she could be discreet
imagine that
I said to myself
That word
Discreet
If she had used it in one of her essays
perhaps
I would have given her an A

Talking Revolution

We know those kinds
We know those kind all too well
They good at talking revolution
They all for and about the revolution
The motherland they say
The reunification of all Africans
Organize
Organize
They say
Our people the world over must become organized
More conscious
This is what they say
You have to watch those kinds
They love the trappings and the lingo
Quoting Malcolm Garvey Nkrumah and Stokely
Slapping hands in comradery
Breaking the bonds they say of mental slavery
For example
They say
We must respect and admire the beauty within our own race
Even as they live comfortably
Unabashedly
Unapologetically
Over on the other side

You have to be careful with those kinds
Those kinds can lead you down the path
Of conviction
Commitment
Yes
Even to a higher level of consciousness
Yet get you locked up or even worse

Even as they walk in dark stark contradiction
They say they will give up everything for the revolution
That may be true
Only as long it does not include the bottle
And those other shades of women

The Message Hidden
in the Dance

We walked into the club
And there I saw her but not before she saw me
Made me her intended target
Her next victim
She didn't even have to stalk me
We hit the floor
We started to dance
We danced for awhile
She even said she loved my style
I was dancing
All in to it
She was sending a message to her man

We danced
I could scarcely keep up
She was moving all across the floor
It was sensual
I was just happy
To be along for the ride
I thought she really liked my style
So
Like I said

I was dancing
All in to it
She was sending a message to her man

We went high
We went low
She dipped
And did a twirl
I thought to myself
Man this is getting serious
After that dip and a twirl
I was beginning to really dig her style
That's when I really started dancing
Yes
I was dancing
All in to it
She was sending a message to her man

I started to sweat
She was glistening
Scintillating
Tantalizing
Visions of what this evening could become started swirling
around in my head
We danced for quite a while
I thought we were digging each other's style
From my perspective
There was no doubt about it

I was dancing
All in to it
She was sending a message to her man

We did the Jerk
We did the Split
The Bump
The Watoozie
The Funky Chicken
The Mashed Potato
We did the Twist
Mustang Sally
The Alligator
Then she turned and did the Feather
What was left for me to do
Except make a fool of myself
So I kicked it up another gear
I was dancing
All in to it
She was simply sending a message to her man

Just when I was about to pop the question
He came over
Gave her a little pinch
Clearly
He had received the message
As for me
Well
I was just happy to have been there that night for the assist

Junkanoo

They say
Everywhere I go
They always say
Tell us about Junkanoo
And then I have to stop
Pause
Ponder for a moment
Then I commence
Junkanoo
Jukanoo
Junkanoo is a celebration
A celebration of life
A celebration of freedom
A celebration of life and freedom as we know it
It's rhythmical
hypnotic
It is a triumph of a people's imagination and creativity
An expression
An expression of who we are
From whence we came
And what we've carved out of life's experiences
Our experience
The bitter and the sweet
From the pulsating rhythm

The colors

The names

The collection of sounds

To the dance

Junkanoo

What is it

It's an expression of liberation

A proud moment

To show to the world Africa and what she has wrought

Take for example the drums

Africa gave us the gift of the drum

The beat

Even a flare for color and pageantry

Then we made the colors even more vibrant and bold

Made them our own

Reflective of another world and all that resides in it

We are creators you see

Improvisers

We take the cowbells

Mixed in the Whistles

To create a new sound

The sound

Still evolving

Reflecting life anew

Expressing a new dance with life

A new beat

Then we mix in the themes that is life

Religions

Natural beauty
Our history
Politics
Even world affairs
They all come to life and on display for the world to see
The world showed us a horn
We embraced it
We took it and added it to the beat the rhythm
Not to out-do the drums
For that's who we are
We are creators
Improvisers
Melody makers
Naturally gifted and rhythmical
We even gave it a name
A name like no other
We called it Junkanoo
There is nothing else like it
People come from all around
To see it in all its glory and majesty
Pulsating to the bones
The beat
That sound
When you hear it
You just can't sit down
It is wild syncopated joyous sensual and free
It's a new dance
A new rhythm

It's an old dance
An old rhythm
We just celebrate it in a new place
In a new way
And
Proudly claim it as our own

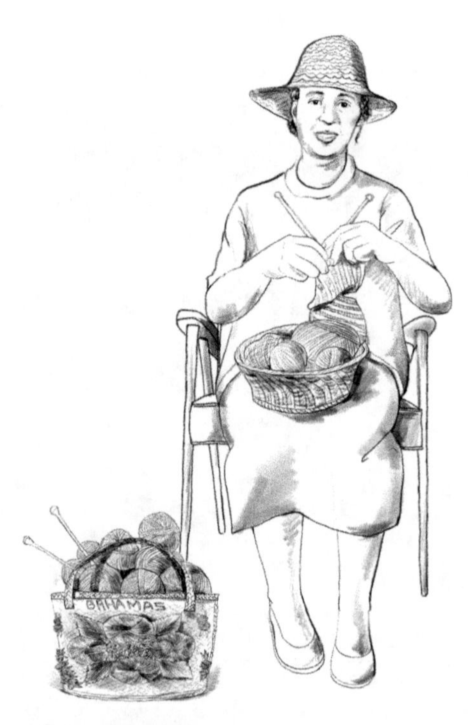

BAHAMAS

A Strong Black Woman

My life has been blessed
And enriched
By the women in my life
I have none other than God to thank for that
Take my mom for example
Every time I read Proverbs thirty one
I see a picture of my mom
Like the lady in that famous chapter of that famous book
Who was virtuous for true
Yet so much more
In the same way
My mom too was hard to fathom and define
Virtuous for true
Yet she was so much more
She was that wife
Never looking to upstage
She was quiet
Yet discerning
Resourceful
Hardworking
Full of faith
Strong
Loving and tough
In the absence of my dad

Whenever he was away
She didn't wait
She just carried on
She used to tell the story of how they met
And got married at an early age
She was from Kemp's Bay
My dad from the settlement below
My dad had to leave
Go on fishing and sponging trips
He still had many mouths to feed
They had no place to stay
So she took a cutlass and cleared down
The acre of land they were to live on
Then she piled up rocks for the foundation
My mom was resourceful
Industrious
Smart
There was nothing she could not do
She didn't have time for idleness or confusion
She plied the gifts God gave her
Her only tool was her hand
For example my mom would use the straw from the coconut
tree
From which she would make purses
Hats
And hand bags
She had a home-made display for her wares that she made
Hats of all description

Small handbags
Baskets
Ladies purses
Speckled with gems of sea shells that cluttered the shoreline
Each and every one of her creation was an act of love
An intricate work of art
Her most loyal customers were the few tourists
And the out of towners that came through
They would gawk admiringly at my mom's handy work
And go, you made that
And where did you learn to do all that
Whenever my dad came home she always had a surprise for him
sometimes ten
twenty
Sometimes forty dollars
That she had produced from her own small private enterprise
My mom cared for all nine of us
My dad was mostly gone
Or he was busy
Well respected in all of the surrounding settlements
She had several of the local women in her employ
They would wash and iron the clothes
She would never let anyone work for free
That was beneath her dignity
She would in all the busyness
Still find time to discipline us
Teach us
She would teach us how to plait

Make baskets and hats
How to cook
She was an excellent cook
When she would bake Tarts or Coconut or Benny Cakes
She would feed the neighborhood kids over the fence
She taught all of us to iron
to wash
And how to turn the beds down
Then at night
As she tucked us in
She would pinch us and tickle us
Long enough
To make us cackle
Then she would pat our heads
And say
Alright now go to sleep
Your dad may be coming home tomorrow
My mom
Looking back
She was much more than it seemed
She was a consummate leader
And
In her own way
And in her own right
She was that lady in Proverbs thirty one

How a Boy Became a Man

And she would say
Go then
Leave
Don't stay
That's all you know how to do anyway
Run away
As soon as it gets a little bit bumpy
Those words
And I would pause
Hand still on the knob
Turn
Slowly
Go to her
Over by the window
With the curtain
Drenched in the moonlight
Glimpse the trail of tears upon her cheek
She would turn away
Recoiling
And that part of me
That stubborn part of me would die a little
Melt away a little

Crumble
Breaking up inside
In that fleeting moment I learned
It's impossible
To hurt what you love
Again we fought
Again
she shouted
Go then
Leave
Don't stay
That's all you know how to do anyway
Run away
As soon as it gets a little bit bumpy
Again
pause
Fingers slowly letting go of the knob
The voice inside my head
Saying
Go to her
Over by the window
With the curtain
Drenched in the moonlight
And I would
Glimpse the trail of tears upon her cheek
As she turned away
Recoiling
And that part of me

that I hated
Would die a little bit more
Again we fought
This time
She flung the words at me
Go then
Leave
Don't stay
That's all you know how to do anyway
Run away
As soon as it gets a little bit bumpy
Then the final time
My mind made up
This time she spat them
With venomous spite
I had made it as far as the landing
Go then
Leave
Don't stay
That's all you know how to do anyway
Run away
As soon as it gets a little bit bumpy
I paused
Hating myself for the suspension
Indecision
Felt myself yielding
Letting go
Falling

Abandoning that part of me that I was beginning to loathe
The door
Creaking
Ever so slowly
For the final time
I went over to her
Over by the window
With the curtain
Drenched in the moonlight
Kissed the trail of tears
Felt her trembling
Unyielding
Sobbing
Slowly melting
She clung to me
We clung to each other
And that part of me died
I knew
Forever
And I never heard those words again

My Four Sisters

My four sisters
Love them to death
They all could be counselors and advisors
Beautiful
Talented
Elegant
Sensitive
Kind
Decent
Reasonable
Hardworking
Resourceful
And smart
In all things except men

My Two Daughters

They are the reason
The reason I rise
Walk circumspectly
Tall
Dare not stumble or fail at integrity
Choose where I go
Who I spend time with
My two daughters
They are the reason I rise
Brave the snow
And so much headwind
Life in the pond can sometimes be a struggle
They are the reason
I steer clear of hurting
Disappointing
In so many ways
They are an extension of my wife
My life
Two beautiful reasons
My two daughters

They Say

They say
We must follow our instincts
I say
I will follow Him
They say
We are creatures of habit
I say
I strive to be a creature of faith
They say
We were born to win
I say
We all can win by serving
They say
Success is in the accumulation of things
I say
Success is the fulfilment of purpose
They say
A full life has to do with longevity
I say
Just let me die empty
They say through their actions
That we are the leaders
Here for you to serve us
I say

Didn't I read somewhere that the greatest of all
Came to serve
They say
Seeing is believing
I say
There is a whole lot more to life than we can see
They say
We are all masters of our own fate
I want to say
Where did you learn that?
They say
It's a dog eat dog world
One thing I know for sure
I ain't no dog

I Just Want to Be Happy

My wife
She is not one for hinting at fears
Or dropping thoughts of insecurities
Yet in a rare moment of vulnerability
For fear of the direction
Our relationship was turning
Chasing money
I wanted it all
Right now
Right then
She said
I just want to be happy
My wife is one of the most courageous women I know
She gets it from her mom
Left the islands
With three grown-up children
Leaving behind so many fond memories
A trail of failed attempts at mending a perfect dream
My wife's experiences were not my own
Unlike anything I had ever known
Though we both swam
In the same shallow waters
I couldn't bring myself to hurt her
This she understands

So
Just like the woman I first met
She knows how to melt me
Hedge her bet
Knowing that I can never will it
Having seen so much wreckage
The chases
So much wastes
Vanity
A chasing after the wind
Now
It had brought her to this place
An almost peaceful resignation
A realization
She said
I just want to be happy

Do It Again

My oldest daughter
Around about the age of two or three
She used to like it when I would come home
No matter what time
From work
And hoist her
Heave her toward the ceiling
And she would say
Dad
Do it again
And no matter how many times
Or how fatigued
I would find the strength
To oblige my daughter
Her joy
That confidence
At that hour
Meant all the world to me

A Successful Marriage

This one is tricky
And illusive
Yet
I will go out on a limb
Say with confidence
That I believe it starts and ends with me
I believe
The key to a successful marriage
Can be found in these four simple words
Husbands love your wife
Why
Because
To love is to give
To give is to love
It's all about giving
Loving
I have come to learn that I can't give enough giving
Loving
Giving
physically
Tenderly
Emotionally
Intellectually
I have also had to learn the hard way

It's the action that triggers the reaction

It all begins and ends with me

Caring

Anticipating

What does she want

Before she wants it

I try to provide it

That's caring

So

I have committed my life to being a giver

Whatever she needs I try to provide

I try to make time

To cultivate

To listen

And to teach

To submit

But mainly to love

To give

Loving

Giving

That's what it is all about

One last thing

Then I will close

I have come to learn it is advantageous to give

Because everything I give to her she takes it and multiplies it

Everything

Good or bad

All I am saying is this

Brothers
You to need to be careful
Learn from my advice
Give to her for such is love
But
Please
Be careful what you give to her
Because everything you give to her
She takes it and multiplies it

Send Me

Helpless
Battered and bruised
Almost unrecognizable
Beneath the dirt
And the muck
The mud
And the clay
That's the state that triggered grace
I believe
He looked down
Saw the faint imprint of His name
Still there on the product
His most cherished creation
Filled equally with sadness joy and oh such love
He looked down
I have read somewhere
That sometimes He will act
Just for the reputation of His name
That is why
I believe
I heard Him say
Come now
For the joy that is set before us
Who will go for us

And
I saw my Lord
Heard Him say
Yes
I can see it
I can see the joy
That is set before me
Lord
I want to be that servant
I will go
Send Me

The Devil and
Our Potential

Make no mistake about it

It's not only God who knows

The Devil

He too knows our potential

Not only does he know our potential

He also knows to whom we belong

The Devil had a billion targets

Yet he chose Job

The devil

He is relentless

Stalks us

Dogs us

Taunts us

His mission in life is to divert us from our paths

He is not to be underestimated

Or ignored

Why

Because the Devil knows our potential

And to whom we belong

We Must Rise Above

I am a firm believer
The past
Holding on to it
Never letting go
Can keep one in chains
In bondage
We must learn
We have to try
Try to rise above the past
Above the pain
The hurt
Even the hate
That litter and mark
Indelibly the path we have trod
The past
With all its pain
And hurt
Can weigh us down
ensnare us
Trap us
Frustrate us
Keep us in a state of anger
Un-forgiveness
Incapable of giving and receiving love

We must strive

Always

To live

Beyond life's circumstances

Past and present

How long will we try to navigate

Staring at life in the rear view mirror

No we cannot

Nor should we be dismissive

Or even try to forget

But

We must strive

Always

To rise above our past

If we want to be truly free

One of the Effects
of Slavery

One of the effects of slavery
Was how our father
Who loved us dearly
Who taught us everything he knew and could
But he learned the way of discipline from his father
Who learned it from his father
Who learned it from his
Who learned it from his slave master
It all comes down through generations
Imagine
Learning how to discipline a son or a daughter
From a slave master
The kind of man
Who snatched babies from a mother's arms
In the hole of a ship as it sits in the Nassau Harbor
Un-daunted
Un-phased
Un-moved
By the shrieks and the sobbing of some poor mother
What monster would snatch a new-born baby
From a mother's arm
Un-daunted

Un-phased
un-moved
And feed it to the sharks in the harbor just for recreation
Sometimes when my father would beat us
I swear
I thought he was trying to kill us

Sometimes

Sometimes
I feel that my wife is that better part of me
The only voice I cannot resist
She's oftentimes bigger
more mature
She speaks to me
Softly
Sometimes
Ever so softly
When I am tired
Angry
Beat up
My wife
She speaks to me
Softly
Sometimes
Ever so softly
When I am tired
Angry
Just plain old angry
Inexplicably angry
Sometimes you just feel angry
Beat up
That's when my wife

She speaks to me
Softly
Ever so softly
My wife
She is like my conscience

Only God Can Do That

Even when I was back in the puddle
Long before I came to the pond
I would step out onto the bay
The beach and the ocean and the world
They would stretch out before me
like a canvas
The most magnificent sight to behold
I would gaze out over the horizon
the crystal clear blue waters
the long stretch of beach
I would take in a deep breath
And say to myself
Only God can do that

There Is Nothing Like Discovery

To walk with God is to get to know Him
He whispers
A little more each time
A little more of His eternal plan
Interwoven with our own
To walk with God
To sit
To talk
He loves us
Delights in sharing
Giving
Loving
He wants to tell us
His secrets
Our secret
In the quiet
Through the storm
Before
During
Even after
He whispers
Secrets

The secret touching us
To walk with God is to get to know Him
He whispers
A little more each time
A little more of His eternal plan
Interwoven with our own
The more we spend time in His presence

Responsibility and Purpose

We are released into responsibility for the purpose of
responsibility
There is something
I believe
God is trying to tell us
Teach us
Here He says
I will give you just a little bit
Now Let me see
What you will do with it
A little taste of what we say
A little taste Of responsibility He says
Something to manage
Something to appreciate
Then
He continues
Now He says
Show me what you can do with the little bit
Before I release to you the rest

God's Grace

I am thinking one day
And I am thinking to myself...
Where could I have been
Where would I have been if it wasn't for Him
Strung out
Lost and confused
In jail
Rudderless
Directionless
Dead
Any of those possibilities
Like so many I knew coming up
We swam together
Like fish
In the shallows
In the puddle
Until
That is
I was hoisted
By His hand
Carried away
To the pond
Away from the corruption and the violence
To my own Egypt

God's grace
Truly His wonderful matchless grace
Where could I have been
Or
Where would I have been if it wasn't for Him

There Is a Place for Unity

Yes
There is a place for unity
But let's not be deceived
It's not just on the basis of race
Sex
Nationality
Ethnicity
Religion
Or any other
Yet
There is a place for unity
For confrontation
Even for waging war
Fight
We should fight
Put up the good fight
But
Let us first define the enemy
Reflecting on life
I do not see where life for us was ever meant to be a competition
So we must not be deceived ever
We must band together to fight the enemy

A real enemy
The enemy
The one true enemy
Our enemy is not each other
The enemy of life is ignorance

Liberation

In the words of William Shakespeare
All's well
That ends well
And I guess that is true
Of my four sisters
They have found the strength to carry on
To find peace
Joy
And happiness
Even after regrets
My two oldest
They are twins
They have found it in their families
Children and grandchildren
My next to the oldest
She remarried
She made sure he was committed and submitted
Good for her
My youngest sister
She is one of my greatest inspirations
God has blessed her
She knows what it means to be truly free
Free of impulsive and compulsive men
Free of anger

Free of confusion
Free of debt
Free to be who and what God wants her to be
Free
Today
It's owning and operating a school
My four sisters
Their lives could have ended back there somewhere
They chose instead
To turn the page
Start a new chapter
And
With the help of the Almighty God
Rewrite their stories

Creation

Creation
The world around us
that speaks
that shouts
sometimes shrieks
quietly
that proclaims
that announces
that tells a story
that reflects
that testifies
that sings
quietly
that whispers
That inspires us
Creation
The world around us
Captivating
Living and breathing
That takes our breath away
Like a painting
The blue sky like a canopy
The ocean
The darker shade of blue

Where ocean and sky tend to meet
The trees in the forest
The majestic rolling undulating hills
The mountains crowned with snow
Once in a while snorting angrily
The thunder clap
The lightning lighting up the sky
Terrifying
From storm to calm
From calm to fury
Night fades to day
The sun rises and sets without delay
The seasons come and go
The tick tock of time itself
The wind
it sometimes roars
Sometimes it whispers
The evenings and the mornings
The setting of the sun and its rising
Ever so consistent
Faithful like nothing else
The grandeur
The beauty
The vastness
The order of it all
The fields ablaze with colors
The animals well fed
Romping and at play

ever so cavalierly
Birds chirping
A symphony of praise it seems
Creation
It speaks
It shrieks
It shouts
It proclaims
It announces
Ever so quietly
It tells a story
A story of purpose and order
It reflects
It testifies
It sings
It whispers
Loud and clear
It says
God

Meant for Each Other

You were my best friend's girl
But I always thought that we were meant for each other
When he would say hurtful things to you
I would get angry
Deep down inside
Why did you let him do those things to you
And when he would borderline abuse you
On the side of the road
When we were out late at night
Pretending to be serious about catching crab
But only because our parents had made us go
So when he would lash out at you
Say the things he always said to you
On the side of the road
I would feel the blows too
He proved me right
Maybe he proved both of us right
I could see the way you looked at me
Abashed and ashamed
He did you wrong
All the while I had to live with the regret
All I could do was watch in that sly and slanted way
And commiserate
Pine

And pine away
Knowing
Believing
Knowing it wouldn't last
But you were his girl
And he was
After all
My best friend
This was back there
In our small world of Andros
Walking the lonely dark road
Pretending to be serious about catching crab
But only because our parents had made us go
This was back when knowing was believing
And believing knowing
Knowing
I just knew it would end that way
Some day
Me
Knowing
That the two of us
Were meant for each other

When It Comes to Family

Families are like glass
Precious
Beautiful
Fragile
Easily broken
Most of the time they are fun to be around
To reminisce with
And reflect
But sometimes they break
Or get broken
Sometimes they come broken
Or they get broken in ways that can make you angry
Can't be mended
And you want to discard them
But that is where the comparisons end
Because you don't get to choose your family
They just come
Like Scorpio

We all know that Scorpio was broken in some way
But we can't help it
There is nothing anybody can do
You don't get to choose your family
Like you do with a piece of chandelier
Sometimes

They just come like Scorpio
Broken
And you have to love them
Love them anyway
You can't throw them away
Even though there are times when you want to
You can't discard them
Because the brokenness is nobody's fault
You just have to love them

My other family members
The ones who sound distant to me
And far away
Ever so far away
They say
You can love family
Yes you can
And you should love family
But sometimes you have to love them from afar
This is what my other family members say
The ones who sound distant to me
And far away
Ever so far away
They say
Sometimes
You just have to love certain family members from afar
But I don't know what that means
And then I think of Scorpio

In the Morning (In the Corner of My Little Room)

When I rise
And before I open my door to peek out
Step out into the world
Before I head into the head wind
That can be ever so strong
So cold
So indifferent
I step into my little room
In the tight space of the narrow corner
To meet with Him there
To greet Him and say to Him thank You
Give Him praise
Pour out my heart
Tell Him about all my hurts
My aches
My pain
And thank Him some more
To praise Him
And thank Him some more
My Heavenly Father
For my life

My family
The gift He has given to me
And I thank Him even for the head wind
He knows my every thought
My every care
What's on my mind and in my heart
Even before they touch my lips
I just know He does
My Heavenly Father
My spirit confirms it
And I am happy
Happy just to know
That He is happy that I took the time
To meet with Him there
In the corner of my little room

I Used to Think

I use to think
The world was a puddle
And the puddle the world
No one could tell me different
Early at the university
We would sit and have those discussions
Intense
Heated discussions
The Puddle
You would say
Try to convince me
The Puddle was Third World
A poor country
Not The Puddle I would say
You must be joking
And I would take out my sword and want to fight like Don
Quixote
That is until I saw the connectedness
Nassau
Kingston
Trinidad and Tobago
Rio
Havana
Atlanta

Soweto

Lagos

Accra

Nairobi

And Cairo

That is until I met

Du bois

Williamson

Lumumba

Sojourner Truth

Nkrumah

Cabral

Garvey

Rodney

King

Harriet Tubman

Douglas

Malcolm

And Sekou Toure

And They Will Say…

And they will say
Tell us
Where you from again
And I will say
Andros
I am from Andros
And they will laugh
An all too familiar laugh
And go
Andros…
And I will say
Yes
I am from Andros
I am from the island of Andros
Andros is home to me
Swimming in the blue hole
Running
Chasing
Running
Skipping
Playing
Skylarking around with my friends along white sandy beaches
Yes, I am from the island of Andros

Andros is home to me
Andros
That sun-drenched land
Where it rains sometimes in the summer time
And the coconut trees sway gently in the sweet cool breeze

About the Author

Bertram Smith is an educator and lives, along with his darling wife, Leslie in Atlanta, Georgia. He has worked in several major industries in a slew of jobs since leaving the Bahamas in 1980. His primary work and career has been in the field of education. He has taught in the public school system in Gwinnett County for over twenty years. He has been an adjunct professor at the New Orleans Baptist Theological Seminary and Lovell college. He has also worked as a regional coordinator for the Lesley University cohort system in the Atlanta metropolitan area.

Bertram has also served in many capacities in church life including assistant pastor, minister of education, minister of evangelism and outreach, and Sunday school teacher. He is the proud father of two beautiful daughters, Falashade and Jamani.

Some of Bertram's passions include, preaching, teaching, reading, cooking, fishing, and spending time with his family.

www.ingramcontent.com/pod-product-compliance
Lightning Source LLC
Chambersburg PA
CBHW061738050726
47598CB00002B/537